20 Hands-On Activities for
Learning
Idioms

by Michael Gravois

SCHOLASTIC
PROFESSIONAL BOOKS

New York ♦ Toronto ♦ London ♦ Auckland ♦ Sydney ♦ Mexico City ♦ New Delhi ♦ Hong Kong ♦ Buenos Aires

burn the candle at both ends   wear your heart on your sleeve   save for a rainy day   apple of your eye   mad as a wet hen   pull a rabbit out of a hat   on cloud nine   barking up the wrong tree   fat cat

Dedication

To my girls

MyDonna for being such a positive influence on the students she teaches, and Wendula for patiently waiting to be included in a dedication

To use an idiom, "You are the apples of my eye!"

Cover design by Kelli Thompson

Interior design by Ellen Matlach Hassell
for Boultinghouse & Boultinghouse, Inc.

Interior illustrations by Teresa Anderko,
Ellen Matlach Hassell, and Manuel Rivera

ISBN 0-439-18723-0

Contents

Introduction

About the Book

There are thousands of idioms in the English language, and students will run across them regularly in their readings, in conversation, or when watching television. When taken literally, idioms do not make much sense. However, these seemingly nonsensical phrases carry hidden meanings, and the study of them will help your students understand metaphors, find the relationships between language and life experience, and discover the fun of wordplay.

New idioms are constantly appearing in the English language (for example, *give me five*, or *going channel surfing*). When they first appear, they are novel and unique, and often become popular quickly. However, before too long, they become clichés, something to be avoided in our own writing. By putting a new twist or spin on an old idiom one's writing can become clearer and more colorful.

The projects and activities in this book are meant to help you teach the understanding of idioms in a fun, hands-on way, making your lessons unique and varied, and engaging your students in their learning. I have used many of the activities included in this book in my own second- and fifth-grade classrooms, and have found that they tap into the different learning styles of my students. The projects, the discussions of wordplay, and the dramatic activities help the students think creatively and leave them laughing. And as we know, *laughter is the best medicine.*

How to Use the Book

Many of the projects featured in this book can be used when studying topics from across the curriculum, thereby linking the study of idioms to subjects other than language arts. At the start of most activities, you will find cross-curricular suggestions, but feel free to build your own bridges.

There are many ways to introduce the meanings of idioms to your students. I have used several methods over the years:

Brainstorming and Webbing   Sometimes the meaning of an idiom is obvious or well-known, in which case you can ask students to explain its meaning or use it in a sentence. When an idiom is not as well-known, write it on the board and ask the class to brainstorm its possible meaning. First, discuss the reasons why students think it has the meaning they've suggested. Then reveal the idiom's true meaning.

butterflies in the stomach · bolt from the blue · go fly a kite · like two peas in a pod · let the cat out of the bag · behind the eight ball · keep it under your hat · back to square one · open a can of worms

Using It in a Sentence   Another way to get students to guess an idiom's meaning is to use it in a sentence yourself or describe a situation. The students will use context clues to make suggestions about the idiom's meaning.

Group Activities   Divide the class into groups of four and say an idiom aloud. Each group has to agree on a meaning for the idiom and write it down. Ask groups to reveal their meanings aloud. Any group guessing it right gets a point. Discuss the real meaning of the idiom and continue playing the game. The group with the most points at the end of the game wins.

Bluffing Game   Divide the class into groups of three or four. (A total of seven groups works well.) Read an idiom aloud. Each group should agree on a meaning for the idiom and write it down. Collect the meanings but do not read them aloud yet. Any group that gets it right gets two points (and they don't play the next part of the game). Put the correct guesses aside. Then read the other guesses (including the correct meaning) in random order. The groups who did not receive two points should write down the number of the meaning that they believe is the correct one. The groups then reveal their guess and receive one point if they are correct. Try this for ten different idioms. The group with the most points at the end of the game wins.

Using the *Scholastic Dictionary of Idioms*   The *Scholastic Dictionary of Idioms* by Marvin Terban (Scholastic, 1996) is a wonderful idiom resource for your classroom. It features more than six hundred idioms, their meanings, and their origins. When completing some of the projects or playing some of the games included in this book, allow students to consult the dictionary for the meaning of any idiom with which they are not familiar.

Your Heart's in the Right Place: Heart-Shaped Accordion Books

Have your students create heart-shaped accordion books as they study the meanings of heart-related idioms. This activity is a perfect language arts companion to a unit on the heart, the circulatory system, feelings, or *Romeo and Juliet*.

Idioms

- ♦ **Bleeding heart**
- ♦ **Eat your heart out**
- ♦ **Have your heart in your mouth**
- ♦ **Wear your heart on your sleeve**
- ♦ **Your heart's in the right place**

What to Do

MATERIALS
- copies of the accordion book template (page 7)
- scissors
- tape
- colored pencils

1. Give each student a copy of the template.
2. Direct them to trim off the edges along the solid rectangle and then cut the template in half along the solid line.
3. Next, have them tape the two strips of paper end-to-end so they form one long strip (panel 4 following panel 3). The tape should be placed on the back side of the strip (opposite from the writing).
4. Instruct students to fold the strip accordion-style along the dotted lines so that panel 1 is on the top.
5. With the accordion book folded, have students cut out the heart shape on the cover so that all six panels are cut. The book can now be opened up into a "paper-doll" chain of hearts.
6. Students should then reverse-fold the accordion book so that the six panels with writing are on the inside of the book.
7. Have students write two heart-related idioms on panels 1 and 4.
8. On panels 2 and 5, students should use their own words to explain the meaning of the two idioms.
9. On panels 3 and 6, they should draw and color a picture illustrating the meanings of the two idioms.
10. Finally, have students write a title for their accordion book on the cover using creative lettering. They can then decorate the cover.

Try This Idea!

Create a 3-D bulletin board by stapling panels 1 and 6 to the bulletin board and allowing the other panels to stand out. Add a banner that says "Idioms From the Heart."

Heart-Shaped Accordion Book Template

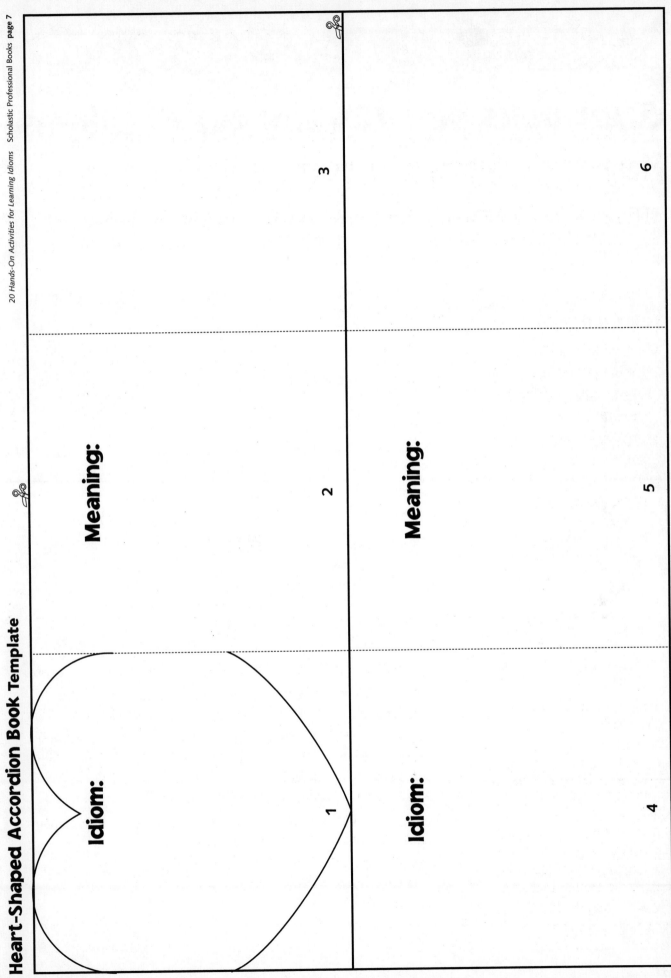

Idiom:

Meaning:

1

2

3

Idiom:

Meaning:

4

5

6

Sunbooks for "Every-day" Idioms

When they first appear, idioms are novel and unique. Over time, their origins often are lost or forgotten. Brighten up your classroom with a vibrant, spinning display of sunbooks that encourage your students to learn about the origins of idioms.

Idioms

- ♦ Call it a day
- ♦ Dog days of summer
- ♦ Field day
- ♦ Red-letter day
- ♦ Rome was not built in a day
- ♦ Save for a rainy day

Try This Idea!

Hang a string across your classroom. Tie pieces of thread of varying lengths along the string. Tie a paper clip to the end of each piece of thread. Paper-clip the tops of each sunbook to the thread to create a long mobile of students' work. When a breeze blows past the sunbooks they spin, creating a vibrant display to jazz up your classroom!

What to Do

MATERIALS
- two copies (on white paper) of the drawing template (page 10) for each student
- two copies (on colored paper, if possible) of the writing template (page 11) for each student
- colored pencils
- scissors
- glue sticks

1. Review the six "day-related" idioms on page 9 with your students. Discuss their meanings, their usage, and their origins.

2. Have each student choose one of the six idioms for which they will construct a sunbook.

3. Give two copies of each template to each student.

4. Each sunbook will have four pages.

   Page 1: Drawing Template Students should use creative lettering to write the idiom on which they will be reporting. Underneath the idiom, have them write in their own words a sentence that explains its meaning.

   Page 2: Writing Template Students should write a complete, detailed paragraph describing the origins of the idiom they chose.

   Page 3: Drawing Template Students should draw a picture that illustrates the idiom's meaning.

   Page 4: Writing Template Students should write a short story that includes the use of the idiom, either in one of the descriptive sentences or in a quote.

5. After students have filled out each of the pages, they should cut out the shapes and follow the directions for constructing the sunbooks (at the bottom of both template pages).

Meanings and Origins of "Every-day" Idioms

The following descriptions are taken from the *Scholastic Dictionary of Idioms* by Marvin Terban (Scholastic, 1996), a wonderful resource that contains more than six hundred idioms and their origins.

Call It a Day

Meaning: to stop work for the day; to bring a project to an end for the time being

Origin: The idea expressed in this idiom is that a certain amount of work is enough for one day. When you've done that amount, you should "call it a day," meaning to declare that you've done a full day's work and that you're stopping.

Dog Days of Summer

Meaning: the hottest and most humid days of summer, usually much of July and August

Origin: In ancient Roman times people who studied astronomy knew that Sirius, the Dog Star, rose and set with the sun during the hottest weeks of the year, July through mid-August. People thought that the heat from the Dog Star combined with the heat from the sun to make those weeks extra hot. That's why people today call this uncomfortable time the "dog days." People tend to get bored and tired at this time because it's so hot outside.

Field Day

Meaning: to have unlimited opportunities; to have it all your own way; to go all out and experience success at something

Origin: In the 1800s people from schools, fire companies, businesses, and other organizations would participate in wholesome outdoor sports on a big playing field. They would play to their heart's content. Soon, to have a field day meant to indulge yourself in any way you wanted. Even today, some schools have a "field day."

Red-Letter Day

Meaning: a day remembered as especially happy and significant

Origin: In medieval times, religious festivals, holidays, and saints' days were printed in red ink on church calendars. (The other days were in black.) The "red-letter days" were the really special ones. Any day remembered because it's particularly pleasant or important can be called a red-letter day no matter what color ink it's printed in on your calendar.

Rome Was Not Built in a Day

Meaning: a difficult or important goal or task cannot be achieved quickly or all at once

Origin: Rome, the beautiful city on the Tiber River in Italy, was the capital of the Roman Empire. It took centuries for Rome to be built to its full glory. There's a lesson in that. If "Rome wasn't built in a day," then you should be willing to persevere when you're working on a project. Major accomplishments don't happen overnight. Two similar proverbs are "where there's a will, there's a way" and "if at first you don't succeed, try, try again."

Save for a Rainy Day

Meaning: to save for a time of need; to put something away for the future

Origin: Since the sixteenth century, "rainy day" has meant a time of need, misfortune, hardship, and affliction. So if things are "sunny" for you now, don't waste everything you have. Put some away for a "rainy day" because circumstances may change.

Sunbooks for "Every-day" Idioms   Drawing Template

Directions

1. In one sun, use creative lettering to write the idiom on which you chose to report. Underneath the idiom, write a sentence that explains its meaning.

2. In the other sun, draw and color a picture that illustrates the idiom's meaning.

Cut out each circle and fold them in half.
Use a glue stick to attach half of the back of a drawing template to half of the back of a writing template. Align along the folds.

Attach the other two templates the same way. Glue all four templates together.

Cut along the rays to make a three-dimensional sun.

20 Hands-On Activities for Learning Idioms   Scholastic Professional Books

Sunbooks for "Every-day" Idioms   ## Writing Template

Directions

1. In one sun, write a complete, detailed paragraph describing the origins of the idiom you chose.

2. In the other sun write a short story that includes the use of the idiom, either in one of the descriptive sentences or in a quote.

Cut out each circle and fold them in half.
Use a glue stick to attach half of the back of a drawing template to half of the back of a writing template. Align along the folds.

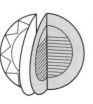

Attach the other two templates the same way. Glue all four templates together.

Cut along the rays to make a three-dimensional sun.

20 Hands-On Activities for Learning Idioms   Scholastic Professional Books

Five Senses Flap Books

During a unit on the five senses have your students create flap books that focus on idioms related to sight, hearing, smell, taste, and touch. See page 15 for a list of these idioms.

What to Do

MATERIALS
- double-sided copies of the five senses template (pages 13 and 14)
- scissors
- stapler
- colored pencils

1. Copy the templates for the flap book back-to-back as they appear in the book. Give one template to each student.

2. Have students cut out the three panels along the thick solid separating lines.

3. Direct students to fold each panel along the dotted line as shown below.

4. Help students slip the panels together so they can see the titles for each panel. Fasten the top of each book with two staples.

5. Students should follow the directions on each of the panels to complete their flap books.

List three things that make you "down in the mouth."

1. _____

2. _____

3. _____

List three things that make you "foam at the mouth."

1. _____

2. _____

3. _____

FOLD

Meanings of Hearing-Related Idioms

—— young, inexperienced, and immature

—— children often hear and understand a lot more than people give them credit for

—— eager to listen; sharply attentive

—— to create something valuable or beautiful out of something worthless or ugly

—— to pay attention and become well-informed

2. Hearing

Idiom

Choose one of the idioms related to the sense of touch and circle it.

- **By the skin of your teeth**
- **Get under your skin**
- **More than one way to skin a cat**
- **No skin off your nose**
- **Touch and go**
- **Wouldn't touch something with a ten-foot pole**

Meaning

In your own words, write the meaning of the idiom you selected.

_____

_____

_____

FOLD

Draw a picture illustrating your description of something that is "a sight for sore eyes."

1. Sight

FOLD

Five Senses Flap Book

Fill in the blanks with the following idioms. Two idioms will not be used.

♦ **Smell a rat**
♦ **Come up smelling like a rose**
♦ **Cut off your nose to spite your face**
♦ **Pay through the nose**
♦ **Follow your nose**
♦ **Make it by a nose**
♦ **Look down your nose at someone**

1. When a severe frost hits Florida, people have to _____ to buy orange juice.

2. You shouldn't _____ just because he or she looks different than you.

3. We're running a little late for the movie, but if we leave now we'll _____ .

4. "Even though you all claim to be innocent, I _____," said the detective.

5. When he asked me the way to the bakery, I said, "_____."

Write the number of each of the idioms from the list below on the line in front of its proper meaning.

1. **All ears**

2. **Keep your ear to the ground**

3. **Little pitchers have big ears**

4. **Make a silk purse out of a sow's ear**

5. **Wet behind the ears**

_____ List three things that "make your mouth water."

1. _____
2. _____
3. _____

List three things that you like to "run off at the mouth" about.

1. _____
2. _____
3. _____

Describe something that you would consider "a sight for sore eyes."

_____
_____
_____

Creative Writing

Write a short story that conveys the meaning of the idiom you selected.

_____
_____
_____
_____
_____
_____

Idioms Related to the Five Senses

Sight

- A sight for sore eyes
- Apple of your eye
- Beauty is in the eye of the beholder
- Eye for an eye and a tooth for a tooth
- Eyes in the back of your head
- More than meets the eye
- Out of sight, out of mind
- Pull the wool over your eyes
- See eye to eye

Hearing

- All ears
- Keep your ear to the ground
- Lend an ear
- Little pitchers have big ears
- Make a silk purse out of a sow's ear
- Wet behind the ears

Touch

- By the skin of your teeth
- Feel your oats
- Get under your skin
- More than one way to skin a cat
- Touch and go
- Won't touch something with a ten-foot pole

Taste

- Born with a silver spoon in your mouth
- Don't look a gift horse in the mouth
- Down in the mouth
- Foam at the mouth
- Hand-to-mouth existence
- Have your heart in your mouth
- Laugh out of the other side of your mouth
- Make your mouth water
- Out of the mouths of babes
- Put your money where your mouth is
- Run off at the mouth
- Straight from the horse's mouth
- Word of mouth
- Zipper your mouth

Smell

- Come up smelling like a rose
- Cut off your nose to spite your face
- Follow your nose
- Keep your nose to the grindstone
- Look down your nose at someone
- Make it by a nose
- No skin off your nose
- Pay through the nose
- Smell a rat
- Smell something fishy
- Turn up your nose at someone

Fire-Idiom Matchbooks

Creativity in your classroom will catch on like wildfire as your students write dialogue while creating matchbooks that feature fire-related idioms. This activity also provides a wonderful opportunity for you to teach fire safety.

Idioms

- ◆ **Add fuel to the fire**
- ◆ **Burn the candle at both ends**
- ◆ **Burn the midnight oil**
- ◆ **Burn your bridges behind you**
- ◆ **Burn yourself out**
- ◆ **Hot under the collar**
- ◆ **On the hot seat**
- ◆ **Out of the frying pan and into the fire**
- ◆ **Play with fire**
- ◆ **Where there's smoke, there's fire**

What to Do

MATERIALS
- copies of the matchbook template (page 17)
- scissors
- glue stick
- colored pencils
- stapler (optional)

1. Give each student a copy of the template.
2. Have them cut out the template along the solid lines.
3. Ask students to place the matchbook in front of them with the writing faceup. Direct them to fold the small bottom strip upward along the solid line and crease it.
4. Then help students fold the top panel down, tuck it under the lower strip, and crease it.
5. On the lower strip of the cover, ask students to use creative lettering to write a fire-related idiom.
6. On the large panel of the cover, they should draw and color a detailed picture that illustrates the meaning of the idiom.
7. Inside the matchbook, there are two panels. In the upper space have students use their own words to explain the meaning of the idiom. In the lower space have students write a short dialogue between two people using the idiom as it would occur in conversation.

Example:

MOTHER: Jimmy, I don't want you playing with Carl anymore since he was caught stealing a candy bar.

JIMMY: But, Mom, he won't do it again.

MOTHER: Where there's smoke, there's fire!

8. Have students cut out the drawing of the matches, fold back the tab, and glue it behind the lower strip.
9. The completed matchbooks can be stapled to a bulletin board under the title "Playing With Fire!" Or, you can have students glue the matchbooks into their notebooks.

Burn the candle at both ends

Fire-Idiom Matchbook Template

Directions

1. Cut out the matchbook and matches along the solid lines.
2. Fold back TAB A on the matches and crease it sharply.
3. Put a small line of glue across TAB A and glue it to the space inside the matchbook.
4. Fold down the top panel of the matchbook along the dotted line to cover the matches.
5. Fold up the small bottom panel along the dotted line.
6. Write the idiom across the front of the bottom panel.
7. On the front of the matchbook, draw and color a picture that illustrates the idiom.
8. Open the matchbook, fold down the matches, and follow the directions written inside.
9. Fold up the matches and close the cover of the matchbook, tucking it behind the lower panel.

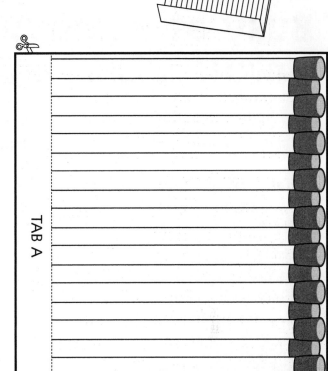

TAB A

USAGE

MEANING

Write a short dialogue between two people that includes the idiom.

Write the meaning of the idiom.

GLUE TAB A HERE.

Busy as a Bee Animal Origami: Animal Idioms and Creative Writing

Your bulletin board will become a virtual zoo as students create construction-paper animals and write creative stories that explain the meanings of animal-related idioms.

Try This Idea!

After each student has created an animal, use thumbtacks to hang the projects on a bulletin board. Create a banner that says "Animal Idioms." If all of the students used the same idiom, such as "busy as a bee," your banner could read "A Swarm of Idioms" or some other related phrase. Curve the banner in and out a few times to give it a wavy, 3-D effect. Tape the banner to the bulletin board wherever it touches.

Snug as a bug in a rug

What to Do

MATERIALS
- copy of the animal-related idioms (page 19)
- copies of the directions (page 20)
- construction paper
- scissors
- colored pencils and markers
- glue sticks

1. Post the list of animal-related idioms in your classroom.

2. Give students the opportunity to choose an animal-related idiom about which they would like to write a short story. Make sure they use the correct meaning of the idiom.

3. Students should select a sheet of construction paper that is the main color of the animal mentioned in the idiom (for example, gray for a mouse, brown for a dog, and so on). Then have them follow the directions on page 20 to create the animal.

4. Before students add details to their animals, instruct them to open up the paper completely. On the inside of their animal, have students use creative lettering to write the idiom they chose. This should be written in the top corner of the paper. Underneath the idiom, have them write a short, creative story using the idiom in its proper context. (See example for the idiom "snug as a bug in a rug," at left.)

5. After students have written their story, they should fold the paper back into the animal shape and add details such as eyes, nose, tail, whiskers, and markings.

Hint: With the directions on page 20, students can create a wide range of animals. Use the list of animal-related idioms on page 19 to spark students' imaginations.

Animal-Related Idioms

- Ants in your pants
- As the crow flies
- Bats in your belfry
- Beat a dead horse
- Bee in your bonnet
- Bird in the hand is worth two in the bush
- Birds of a feather flock together
- Bug off
- Bull in a china shop
- Busy as a beaver/bee
- Butterflies in the stomach
- Buy a pig in a poke
- Cat got your tongue?
- Chicken feed
- Chickens come home to roost
- Clean as a hound's tooth
- Cold turkey
- Cook your goose
- Crocodile tears
- Dark-horse candidate
- Dead as a dodo
- Dead duck
- Dog days of summer
- Dog-eat-dog world
- Dog's life
- Don't count your chickens before they hatch
- Don't look a gift horse in the mouth
- Eager beaver
- Early bird catches the worm
- Eat crow

- Fat cat
- Fish or cut bait
- Fish out of water
- Fly in the ointment
- For the birds
- Get your goat
- Go to the dogs
- Have other fish to fry
- High horse
- Hold your horses
- Horse of a different color
- Kill the goose that lays the golden eggs
- Kill two birds with one stone
- Knee-high to a grasshopper
- Let sleeping dogs lie
- Let the cat out of the bag
- Live high off the hog
- Lock the barn door after the horse is out
- Look what the cat dragged in
- Mad as a wet hen
- Make a silk purse out of a sow's ear
- Monkey business
- More than one way to skin a cat
- No spring chicken
- Open a can of worms
- Play cat and mouse
- Poor as a church mouse
- Pull a rabbit out of a hat

- Put all your ducks in a row
- Put the cart before the horse
- Quiet as a mouse
- Raining cats and dogs
- Rat race
- Rats abandoning a sinking ship
- Red herring
- Scarce as hen's teeth
- Sick as a dog
- Sitting duck
- Smell a rat
- Snug as a bug in a rug
- Stir up a hornet's nest
- Straight from the horse's mouth
- Swan song
- Take the bull by the horns
- Throw a monkey wrench into the works
- Till the cows come home
- What's good for the goose is good for the gander
- When the cat's away, the mice will play
- White elephant
- Wild-goose chase
- Wolf in sheep's clothing
- You can lead a horse to water but you can't make him drink
- You can't teach an old dog new tricks

Animal-Idiom Origami

Follow the directions below to create an origami animal.

Directions

1. Fold the construction paper diagonally so the short edge meets the long edge as shown.

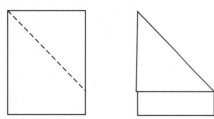

2. Cut off the strip so that a square remains.

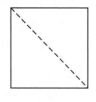

3. Refold the square diagonally.

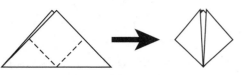

4. Fold the two side points of the triangle to the center point as shown.

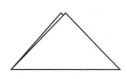

5. Make a curved cut as shown, being sure you are cutting off the open end of the folded paper.

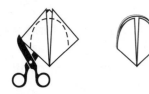

With this base you can make many animals. Depending on the animal you are creating, you may want to reshape it. Here are a few suggestions:

Creating a Bug

Use the animal base as is. The two flaps can be the wings, and a small, round head can be added at the point. Add other details, such as spots or stripes.

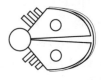

Creating a Mouse

Cut down the two flaps for the ears, as shown by the dotted lines in the figure. Add a tail, eyes, and whiskers.

Creating a Rabbit

The two flaps can be curled under to create floppy ears. Then add eyes and a nose.

Busy as a Beaver:
A Little Book of Animal Idioms

The animal world is filled with creatures possessing unique traits. These traits sparked many idioms that we use to comment on the human experience. Using a twist on the little book format, your students can explore the meanings of these animal-related idioms.

What to Do

MATERIALS
- copy of the animal-related idioms (page 19)
- copies of the directions (page 22)
- white paper
- scissors
- hole puncher
- colored pencils

1. Post the list of animal-related idioms in a central place in your classroom.

2. Give students the opportunity to choose four animal-related idioms to illustrate and write about.

3. Distribute copies of the directions. Have students follow the directions to create their very own Little Book of Animal Idioms.

BIRDS OF A FEATHER
FLOCK TOGETHER

People who have things in common, such as interests and ideas, usually hang out together. This idiom comes from the way birds from the same species gather together in groups.

My Little Book of Animal Idioms

Follow the directions below to create a Little Book to help you explore the meanings of animal-related idioms.

Directions

Part I

1. Fold a sheet of paper in half widthwise.

2. Fold it in half again in the same direction.

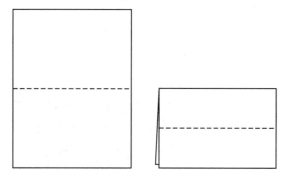

3. Fold this long, narrow strip in half in the opposite direction.

4. Unfold the paper to the position at the end of step 1, and cut halfway along the center fold.

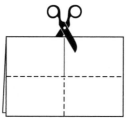

5. Unfold the paper completely. There should be a slit in the center of the paper where you made the cut.

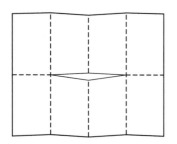

6. Fold the paper in half along the fold with the slit.

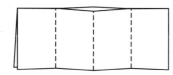

7. Push in on the ends of the paper so the slit opens. Keep pushing until the center panels meet.

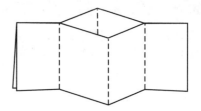

8. Fold the pages to one side to form a book, and crease the edges.

9. Use a hole-puncher to punch two eyeholes through the top three pages as shown.

10. Use the eyeholes as a stencil to draw two circles on the last page of the book. These circles will be the eyes for the animals drawn on each of the pages of the little book. Color in the eyes.

Part II

Once you've created your book template, it's time to fill it in!

1. On each of the inside pages, draw an animal mentioned in three of the four idioms you chose, using the eyes you've created.

2. Under each animal, use creative lettering to write the idiom. On the page below each animal, write a few sentences that explain the meaning of the idiom.

3. On the cover, draw the animal related to the fourth idiom you chose. Personalize your book with a title. On the back cover of the little book, explain the idiom related to the cover illustration.

20 Hands-On Activities for Learning Idioms   Scholastic Professional Books

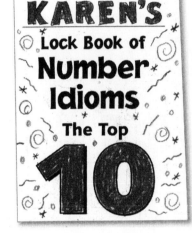

The Top 10:
A Lock Book of Number Idioms

Let the countdown begin as your students explore numerical idioms while creating a lock book that taps into a variety of response styles.

What to Do

MATERIALS • copies of the directions (page 24)
• double-sided copies of the lock book template (pages 25–28)
• scissors
• colored pencils
• world atlas or map
• encyclopedia

1. Copy pages 25 and 26 back-to-back as they appear in the book.

2. Copy pages 27 and 28 back-to-back as they appear in the book.

3. Distribute copies of the directions and the template.

4. Have students follow directions on page 24 and the instructions on each of the panels to complete their lock books.

The Top 10: My Lock Book of Number Idioms

Directions

Part I

1. Cut both pages in half widthwise along the thick solid line. (You will have four half-pages. Discard the blank page.)

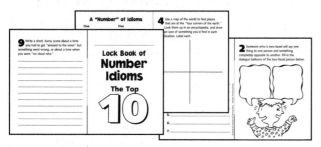

2. Fold the three sheets in half along the center line.

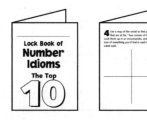

3. Open the pages with the cover and panel 2 and cut along the fold on the solid lines only. The pages will be cut twice, from the outer edges in toward the center along the fold.

4. Open the page with panel 4 and cut along the fold on the solid line only. It may be helpful to first fold the paper in half lengthwise to begin cutting, but be careful not to crease it.

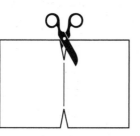

5. Place the page with panel 1 faceup in front of you.

6. Place the page with panel 3 faceup on top of panel 1.

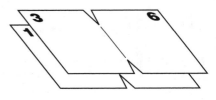

7. Curl the side of the stacked pages and feed them through the slit along the fold between panels 5 and 10.

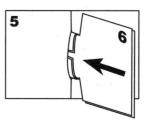

8. Open up the pages so they lock in place.

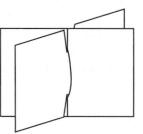

9. Fold the pages into a book shape, making sure they are in the correct order.

Part II

1. Write the possessive form of your name on the line at the top of the cover panel.

2. Color the cover illustration and add any decorations you'd like.

3. Follow the instructions on each of the inside panels to complete your lock book.

20 Hands-On Activities for Learning Idioms   Scholastic Professional Books

9 Write a short, funny scene about a time you had to get "dressed to the nines" but something went wrong, or about a time when you were "on cloud nine."

_____
_____
_____
_____
_____
_____
_____
_____
_____
_____

Lock Book of
Number Idioms

The Top
10

A "Number" of Idioms

One
Once in a blue moon
Once bitten,
   twice shy
One-horse town
One-track mind

Two
Goody-two-shoes
It takes two to tango
Two-faced

Three
Need something like
   a third leg
Two's company,
   three's a crowd

Four
Four corners of
   the earth

Five
Fifth wheel
Give me five

Six
Six of one and a half
   dozen of the other

Seven
Seventh heaven

Eight
Behind the eight ball

Nine
Dressed to the nines
On cloud nine

Ten
Touch something with
   a ten-foot pole

4 Use a map of the world to find places that are at the "four corners of the earth." Look them up in an encyclopedia, and draw an icon of something you'd find in each location. Label each.

1 Choose an idiom from the list under "One" on the back cover. Then draw a one-panel cartoon that conveys its meaning.

8 Being behind the eight ball means you're in trouble or in a difficult position (often due to your own negligence). Write a short dialogue between a teacher and a student that incorporates this idiom.

Teacher: _____

_____

Student: _____

_____

Teacher: _____

_____

Student: _____

_____

Teacher: _____

_____

5 At the end of each finger of the hand below write your favorite thing from each of the listed categories. Write your own category on the thumb.

Give Me Five!

10 Name something from each of the categories below that you wouldn't touch with a ten-foot pole. Be sure to complete the last line with something from a category of your choice.

I wouldn't touch it with a ten-foot pole!

Food: _____

Animal: _____

Activity: _____

Performer: _____

_____ : _____
(Fill in the category.)

7 List seven things that would make you feel as if you were in seventh heaven.

I would be in seventh heaven if . . .

1. _____

2. _____

3. _____

4. _____

5. _____

6. _____

7. _____

20 Hands-On Activities for Learning Idioms   Scholastic Professional Books

2 Someone who is two-faced will say one thing to one person and something completely opposite to another. Fill in the dialogue balloons of the two-faced person below.

3 In your own words, write the meanings of the following two idioms.

Two's company, three's a crowd

_____

_____

_____

_____

Need something like a third leg

_____

_____

_____

_____

_____

6 "Six of one and a half dozen of the other" is an idiom people use when asked to choose between two things they like or dislike equally. Draw pictures of two things you would have trouble choosing between.

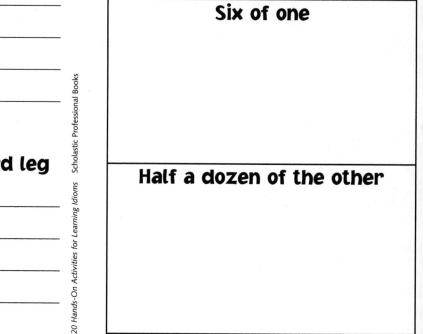

Six of one

Half a dozen of the other

20 Hands-On Activities for Learning Idioms   Scholastic Professional Books

Can't See the Forest for the Trees: Idiom Trees

Have each of your students create an idiom tree that can be tacked onto a bulletin board to create a whole forest of idioms.

What to Do

MATERIALS • copies of the tree templates (pages 30 and 31)
• scissors
• colored pencils
• glue stick

1. Give each student a copy of the templates.

2. Have them cut out the image of the tree and the writing panel.

3. On the chalkboard, write the list of tree-related idioms at right. Ask students to choose one and write it in the rectangle on the front of the tree.

4. On the writing panel, they should write the meaning of the idiom in their own words, and write a quote that uses the idiom in the proper context.

5. After students finish writing, have them color the tree, as well as the leaves above the writing panel.

6. Instruct students to fold the rectangular writing panel along the dotted line (so it closes in on itself) and bend TAB A back along the other dotted line.

7. Have them glue TAB A behind the upper leaves of the tree. When students pull on the leaves above the writing panel, the tree will "grow" to reveal their writing.

Idioms

♦ **Babe in the woods**

♦ **Barking up the wrong tree**

♦ **Can't see the forest for the trees**

♦ **Go climb a tree**

♦ **Out of the woods**

Directions

1. Cut out the outline of the tree.

2. Write the tree-related idiom you selected in the rectangle on the front of the tree.

3. After you finish writing the idiom, color the tree.

4. After coloring the tree, glue the tab on the writing panel behind the top of the tree.

20 Hands-On Activities for Learning Idioms Scholastic Professional Books

Idiom Tree
Writing Template

Meaning

Directions

1. Cut out the outline of the writing template.

2. In your own words, write the meaning of the idiom you chose. Then, write a quote that uses the idiom in the proper context.

3. Fold the writing panel along the dotted line.

4. Fold TAB A back and glue it to the back of the cover template tree top.

Quote

TAB A

Quick on the Draw! Quicksheets

Quicksheets provide a wonderful way to expose your students to a large number of idioms in a short period of time. They also make an attractive hanging display for your classroom.

What to Do

MATERIALS • copies of the template (page 33)
• scissors
• colored pencils
• hole puncher
• string or thread

1. Cut each copy of the template into four separate forms. Give one form to each student.

2. Have students choose an idiom, write it on the top line of the quicksheet, and think of a scenario in which the idiom is used.

3. Next, instruct them to draw and color a picture illustrating the scenario in the box on the quicksheet, as well as write a sentence that uses the idiom in that situation.

4. Have students punch holes in the top of the sheet where indicated.

5. Weave a piece of string or thread through the holes in each of the quicksheets and hang them across your classroom or along one of your classroom walls.

Quick on the Draw!

Quick on the Draw!

Quick on the Draw!

Quick on the Draw!

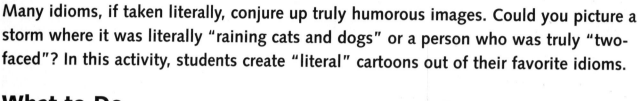

Don't Take It Literally!

Many idioms, if taken literally, conjure up truly humorous images. Could you picture a storm where it was literally "raining cats and dogs" or a person who was truly "two-faced"? In this activity, students create "literal" cartoons out of their favorite idioms.

What to Do

MATERIALS • copies of the template (page 35)
• colored pencils

1. Give each student a copy of the template.

2. Ask students to pick an idiom that conjures up a funny image when taken literally and write the idiom in the space under the title.

3. On the lines, have students write the idiom's actual meaning and a short descriptive paragraph using the idiom properly.

4. In the frame, have them draw a colorful cartoon of the idiom's literal meaning.

5. Hang up the drawings so that everyone can appreciate the humor of idioms.

Suggested Idioms

- Air your dirty laundry in public
- Albatross around your neck
- All ears/thumbs
- Ants in your pants
- At the end of your rope
- Backseat driver
- Bite off more than you can chew
- Bite the dust
- Bite the hand that feeds you
- Bury your head in the sand
- Butter someone up
- Button your lip
- Butterflies in the stomach
- Cat got your tongue?
- Chew up the scenery
- Climb the walls
- Cost an arm and a leg
- Dog's life
- Drive you up the wall

- Eat crow
- Eat your words
- Elbow grease
- Eyes in the back of your head
- Fat cat
- Fifth wheel
- Fly by the seat of your pants
- Follow your nose
- Full of hot air
- Get a kick out of something
- Give your eyeteeth for something
- Go climb a tree/ jump in a lake
- Go over like a lead balloon
- Green thumb
- Green with envy
- Head in the clouds
- Hit the books/ road/roof
- Hold your tongue
- In hot water
- In the doghouse

- Keep your nose to the grindstone
- Knee-high to a grasshopper
- Lay an egg
- Lend an ear
- Little pitchers have big ears
- Long in the tooth
- Mad as a wet hen
- Name is mud
- Need something like a hole in the head
- On pins and needles
- On the ball
- On top of the world
- Open a can of worms
- Pay through the nose
- Pie in the sky
- Play cat and mouse
- Pull your leg
- Pull yourself together
- Put your money where your mouth is
- Raining cats and dogs
- Raise the roof

- Run circles around someone
- Saved by the bell
- Sight for sore eyes
- Skeleton in your closet
- Strike a happy medium
- Sweep you off your feet
- Throw the baby out with the bathwater
- Throw the book at someone
- Till the cows come home
- Too many cooks spoil the broth
- Two-faced
- Walk on eggs
- Walking on air
- Wear your heart on your sleeve
- Wet behind the ears
- Where there's smoke, there's fire
- Wild-goose chase
- Zipper your mouth

Don't Take It Literally!

IDIOM

Meaning:

_____

_____

_____

_____

_____

Using the idiom:

_____

_____

_____

_____

_____

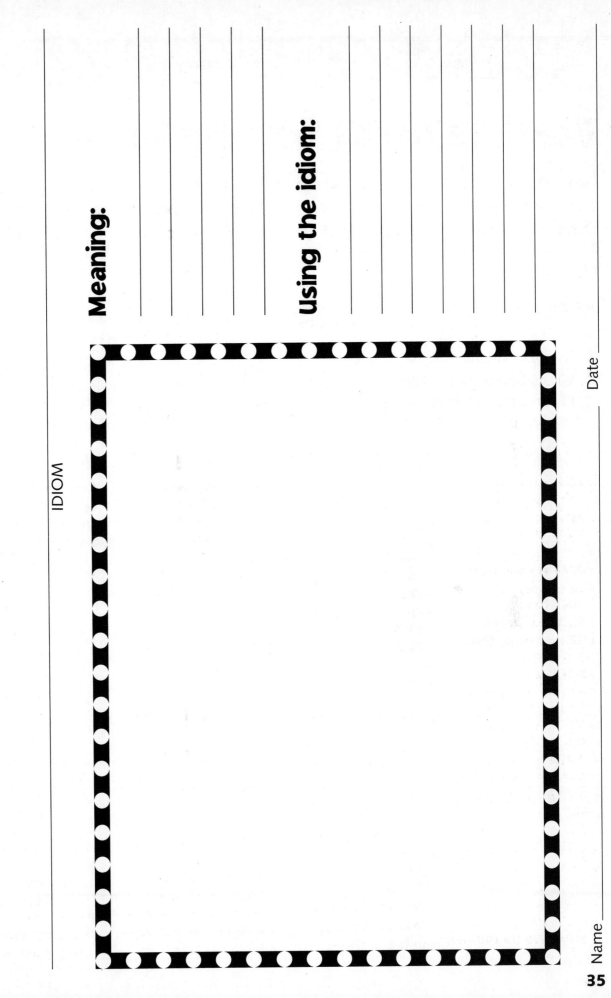

Name _____

Date _____

That's a Horse of a Different Color! Colorful Idioms

Colors often suggest certain feelings, moods, or ideas, and many idioms have developed because of these connotations. In this activity, students explore this concept, and create a colorful troop of horses to gallop across your bulletin board.

Suggested Idioms

Blue
◆ Blue blood
◆ Bolt from the blue
◆ Once in a blue moon
◆ Out of the clear, blue sky
◆ True-blue

Yellow
◆ Go yellow

Red
◆ Catch someone red-handed
◆ Red tape
◆ Red-carpet treatment
◆ Red herring
◆ Red-letter day

White
◆ White elephant

Green
◆ Green thumb
◆ Green with envy

Black
◆ Black sheep of the family
◆ Pot calling the kettle black

Pink
◆ Get the pink slip
◆ In the pink
◆ Tickled pink

Silver
◆ Born with a silver spoon in your mouth
◆ Every cloud has a silver lining

What to Do

MATERIALS
• copies of the horse template (page 37)
• colored pencils
• stapler

1. After explaining the meaning of the idiom "horse of a different color," give each student a copy of the template.

2. Ask students to choose an idiom related to a color of their choice (see the suggestions above), write the idiom in the banner that the rider is holding, and explain its meaning in the space beneath it.

3. Then have them write a quote in the quotation balloon that properly uses the idiom.

4. Students should fill in the horse with the color mentioned in the idiom, but invite them to color the rider however they like.

5. Staple the horses onto a bulletin board and add a banner that reads, "That's a Horse of a Different Color!" Try curving the banner to give it a wavy, 3-D effect, taping it to the bulletin board wherever it touches.

That's a Horse of a Different Color!

Alphabetical Idioms

Surround students with the ABC's of idioms by creating colorful banners, each featuring an idiom beginning with a different letter of the alphabet. Hang the banners around the classroom and expose students to a wide selection of idioms throughout the year.

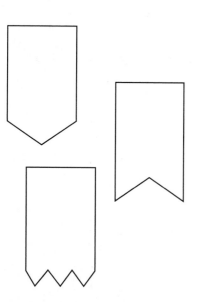

Try This Idea!

Try an oral presentation activity as an alternative to discussing the idioms as you assign the letters. Each student can write a short speech describing the meaning of the idiom they illustrated. Then have the students memorize their speeches and practice the skills associated with public speaking: talking loudly and clearly, and maintaining eye-contact with the audience.

What to Do

MATERIALS
- bulletin board paper in different colors (paper from a 30-inch-wide roll works well)
- scissors
- hat
- white construction paper
- colored markers
- glue stick

1. Cut an 18-inch length from a roll of bulletin board paper for each student.

2. Have students cut the bottom in an interesting shape, such as those shown at left.

3. Start the activity by randomly calling on students or drawing their names from a hat. The first person picked will illustrate the idiom beginning with the letter *A*. Refer to the glossary on page 55 to select an idiom for each letter of the alphabet, except *X*. For *X*, students will have to be creative. For example, encourage them to use a play on words by adapting one of the following egg-related idioms:

    - Put all your X in one basket
    - Walk on X
    - Kill the goose that lays the golden X.

4. Read the idiom and ask the student for its meaning. If the meaning is not clear to the student, ask him or her to share any possible ideas. Then, as a class, discuss its meaning.

5. Continue through the alphabet.

6. Students can illustrate their idiom on a square piece of white construction paper and glue the picture to the banner. Below the picture they should write the upper- and lowercase letter and the idiom they were given. Have students sign their names at the bottom of the banner.

7. Hang students' completed banners around the classroom.

butterflies in the stomach · bolt from the blue · go fly a kite · like two peas in a pod · let the cat out of the bag · behind the eight ball · keep it under your hat · back to square one · open a can of worms

Food for Thought

Give your students some food for thought as they create idiom snacks and write creative stories that tie the idioms together.

Suggested Idioms

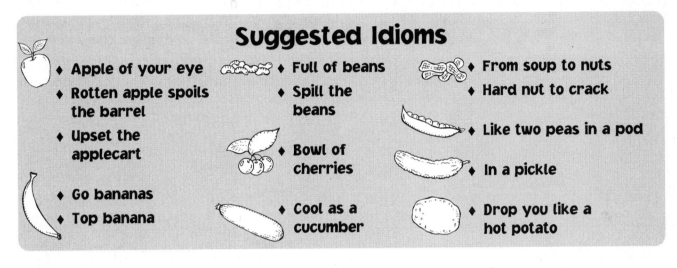

- ◆ **Apple of your eye**
- ◆ **Rotten apple spoils the barrel**
- ◆ **Upset the applecart**
- ◆ **Go bananas**
- ◆ **Top banana**

- ◆ **Full of beans**
- ◆ **Spill the beans**
- ◆ **Bowl of cherries**
- ◆ **Cool as a cucumber**

- ◆ **From soup to nuts**
- ◆ **Hard nut to crack**
- ◆ **Like two peas in a pod**
- ◆ **In a pickle**
- ◆ **Drop you like a hot potato**

What to Do

MATERIALS
- copies of the napkin and food templates (pages 40 and 41)
- scissors
- colored pencils
- glue sticks
- paper plates
- highlighter

1. Give each student a paper plate and a copy of the two templates.

2. Have students choose four idioms from the list above. They should write the related idiom on each piece of food from the food template and color the illustration.

3. Direct them to cut out each food item and use a glue stick to attach it to the paper plate.

4. Ask students to write a creative short story on their "Food for Thought" napkin template that uses the four idioms they chose. If desired, have students use a highlighter to call out each of the idioms in the story. Remind them to sign their names at the end of the story.

5. Finally, have students cut out the napkin template and fold it in half diagonally so it looks like a napkin. They can then cut out the fork and glue it to the napkin as a finishing touch.

Try This Idea!

Staple each student's plate and napkin onto the bulletin board. Create a banner that reads "Food for Thought."

✂--

Food for Thought

_____

_____

_____

_____

_____

_____

_____

_____

_____

_____

_____

_____

_____

_____

_____

_____

_____

Name_____   Date _____

20 Hands-On Activities for Learning Idioms   Scholastic Professional Books

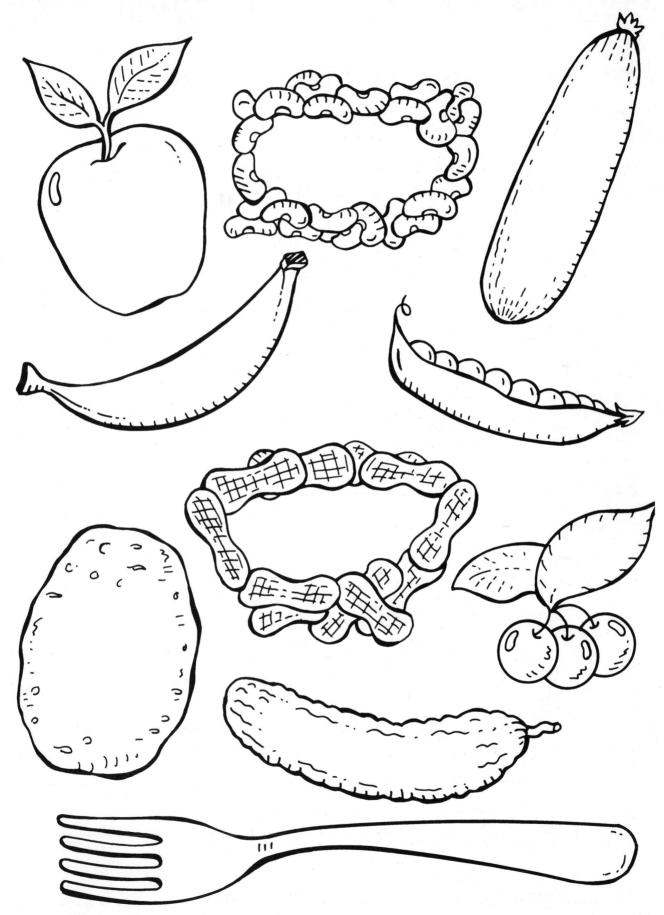

Let the Cat Out of the Bag: Compliment Bags

Everyone loves to receive compliments. Let your students know what their classmates admire most about them by asking your students to "let the cat out of the bag."

What to Do

MATERIALS
- copies of the cat template (page 43)
- paper lunch bags
- hat
- colored pencils
- scissors
- stapler

1. Give each student a paper lunch bag and a copy of the template.

2. Place all of the students' names into a hat, and ask each student to pick a classmate's name. They should not reveal whose name they picked to the other students. (If any student picks his or her own name, ask the student to select again.)

3. On the top line of the cat template, instruct students to write the name of the classmate they picked. Underneath the name, they should write five things that they admire about that person.

4. Invite students to color and cut out the cat. Have them cut around the curved paws of the cat along the white dots—for linking over the top of the lunch bag (see the illustration). Then ask students to write their own names down the front of the paper bag.

5. Staple the bags onto a bulletin board under a banner that reads "(your room) Lets the Cat Out of the Bag." Then let the cats out of the bag by revealing the compliments each of your students wrote about their classmates.

Let the
Cat Out
of the
Bag
Template

Patch-Word Quilt of Preposition Idioms

Integrate the study of idioms into your study of prepositions by creating a large, class-made patch-word quilt bulletin board.

What to Do

MATERIALS
- copies of the directions (page 46)
- 9- by 12-inch construction paper (light colors work best)
- scissors
- glue sticks
- colored markers
- ruler
- stapler

1. Give each student a copy of the directions and two pieces of construction paper.
2. Ask students to choose a preposition-related idiom. (See the suggested idioms on the next page.) Then, have them follow the direction on page 46 to create a quilt patch.
3. After students have finished their patches, staple them next to one another on a bulletin board, alternating colors, to create a large class quilt.
4. Add a banner such as "Patch-Word Prepositions."

Try This Idea!

You can also use this activity to feature other parts of speech. Look through the glossary on page 55 to find idioms that feature verbs, nouns, adjectives, and so on.

Suggested Idioms

Above
- Head and shoulders above someone
- Keep your head above water

Against
- Go against the grain
- Play both ends against the middle
- Up against the wall

Away
- Get away with murder
- When the cat's away, the mice will play

Behind
- Behind the eight ball
- Power behind the throne
- Wet behind the ears

Below
- Below par
- Hit below the belt

Between
- Between a rock and a hard place
- Read between the lines

By
- By the skin of your teeth

Down
- Bring down the house
- Down the drain
- Down the hatch
- Look down your nose at someone

For
- Go along for the ride

In
- Down in the mouth
- In the driver's seat
- In hot water

Of
- Out of sight, out of mind
- Out in left field
- Out of the clear blue sky
- Out of the frying pan, into the fire
- Out of the mouths of babes
- Out of the woods

Off
- Off the beaten track
- Off the top of your head
- Off-the-wall
- Off your rocker

On
- Jump on the bandwagon
- Out on a limb
- Quick (or slow) on the draw

Over
- Over a barrel
- Over the hill
- Over your head

To
- Down-to-the-wire

Under
- Get under your skin
- Take someone under your wing
- Water under the bridge

Up
- Up a creek without a paddle

Patch-Word Quilt of Preposition Idioms

Follow the directions below to create a quilt patch that features a preposition idiom of your choice.

Directions for Making the Quilt Patch

1. Cut a 3-inch strip off two pieces of construction paper, as shown, leaving two 9-inch squares. Then cut one inch off two sides of one square, leaving an 8-inch square.

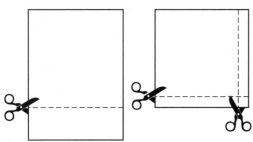

2. Fold the 8-inch square in half diagonally. Then fold it in half again. Unfold the last fold, so the square is still folded in half.

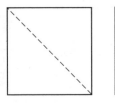

3. Carefully cut along the fold line toward the outside corner. Stop cutting one inch before reaching the corner.

4. Unfold the square and refold along the cut you just made. Repeat step 3, cutting along the remaining fold. Unfold the square. (The cuts form an X in the middle of the square.)

5. Fold the four triangular flaps back and forth. Cut ½ inch off the points of each flap, leaving a square window.

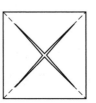

6. Rub a glue stick around the outer edges of the square and glue it in the center of the 9-inch square. The flaps will hide your writing on the construction paper below.

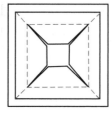

Directions for Writing About the Idiom

1. Choose an idiom containing a preposition to highlight on your quilt patch and write the preposition in the center window of the patch. On the tops of three triangular flaps, write the following labels: Idiom, Meaning, Usage. Write your name on the fourth flap.

2. Under the flap labeled Idiom, write the idiom you selected.

3. Under the flap labeled Meaning, write an explanation of the idiom's meaning.

4. Under the flap labeled Usage, use the idiom in a sentence that conveys the idiom's meaning.

5. Under the flap with your name, write a short description of a way in which the idiom could be applied to some aspect of your life.

For Fun

Decorate the outer border of your quilt patch.

46

Keep It Under Your Hat!

Not only do creative dramatic activities add a spark of fun to your classroom, they also allow students to practice the often-neglected language arts skills of speaking and listening. "Keep It Under Your Hat" is an improvisation game that will start your students thinking creatively—and leave them laughing!

First, explain that "keeping something under your hat" is an idiom that means to keep something secret. Next, divide students into groups of four. Give each group a slip of paper with three different idioms. (You can copy and cut out the lists below.)

Each group should choose one of the three idioms and develop and perform a one-minute scene conveying its meaning. The catch? The idiom cannot be mentioned during the scene; they must "keep it under their hats." Before a group's performance, ask a student from the group write all three idioms on the board. After the scene is completed, invite the audience to guess which of the three idioms was suggested by the performance. You can then discuss the meaning of each of the idioms with the class.

Keep It Under Your Hat!

1. When the cat's away, the mice will play
2. Let the cat out of the bag
3. More than one way to skin a cat

Keep It Under Your Hat!

1. It's a dog's life
2. You can't teach an old dog new tricks
3. Let sleeping dogs lie

Keep It Under Your Hat!

1. Walk on eggs
2. Walking on air
3. Get your walking papers

Keep It Under Your Hat!

1. Water under the bridge
2. Fish out of water
3. In hot water

Keep It Under Your Hat!

1. Make a mountain out of a molehill
2. Make a silk purse out of a sow's ear
3. Make hay while the sun shines

Keep It Under Your Hat!

1. Shake a leg
2. Pull your leg
3. Cost an arm and a leg

Keep It Under Your Hat!

1. You can lead a horse to water but you can't make him drink
2. Put the cart before the horse
3. Lock the barn door after the horse is out

Keep It Under Your Hat!

1. You can catch more flies with honey than with vinegar
2. Early bird catches the worm
3. Catch someone red-handed

Going Back to Square One

Before beginning this activity, explain to students that going "back to square one" is an idiom that means to start something over from the very beginning (often because of a failure to accomplish the desired result). Next, divide the class into groups of four or five. Give each group a slip of paper with a different idiom and ending for the scene. (You can copy and cut out the lists below.)

Using the given ending, each group will "think backward" to develop and perform a scene that would plausibly lead up to that ending. The challenge? The idiom should be one of the last lines in the scene, and the way it is used should convey its meaning.

Before each group's performance, have a group member tell the audience what the ending will be and what idiom was used. Then the class can watch to see how each group solved their problem.

Going Back to Square One

Ending: Swallowing a goldfish

Idiom: Swallow it hook, line, and sinker

The idiom should be one of the last lines in your scene.

Going Back to Square One

Ending: Burning homework you just finished

Idiom: Burn the midnight oil

The idiom should be one of the last lines in your scene.

Going Back to Square One

Ending: Secretly letting a horse out of a fenced-in pasture

Idiom: Straight from the horse's mouth

The idiom should be one of the last lines in your scene.

Going Back to Square One

Ending: Letting your pet rat loose in the teachers' lounge

Idiom: Rats abandoning a sinking ship

The idiom should be one of the last lines in your scene.

Going Back to Square One

Ending: Tearing up a letter

Idiom: Red-letter day

The idiom should be one of the last lines in your scene.

Going Back to Square One

Ending: Selling Grandmother's diamond ring that you promised never to sell

Idiom: Sell like hotcakes

The idiom should be one of the last lines in your scene.

Going Back to Square One

Ending: Throwing out a steak you just cooked

Idiom: Throw the book at someone

The idiom should be one of the last lines in your scene.

Going Back to Square One

Ending: Falling asleep during an important exam

Idiom: Asleep at the switch

The idiom should be one of the last lines in your scene.

One Idiom—Three Situations

Idioms can be used to describe a variety of situations. For this improvisation game, divide students into groups of four or five and assign each group an idiom. Instruct students to develop and perform three short scenes, each one using the given idiom in a different way.

The challenge? The idiom's meaning should be clear in every scene. (You can copy, cut out, and distribute the lists below.) Before each group's performance, read the idiom to the class so they can see how the group solved the problem.

One Idiom: Three Situations

Develop and perform three short scenes that use the idiom below in a unique way.

Idiom: At the end of your rope

One Idiom: Three Situations

Develop and perform three short scenes that use the idiom below in a unique way.

Idiom: Between a rock and a hard place

One Idiom: Three Situations

Develop and perform three short scenes that use the idiom below in a unique way.

Idiom: Early bird catches the worm

One Idiom: Three Situations

Develop and perform three short scenes that use the idiom below in a unique way.

Idiom: Face the music

One Idiom: Three Situations

Develop and perform three short scenes that use the idiom below in a unique way.

Idiom: Bark up the wrong tree

One Idiom: Three Situations

Develop and perform three short scenes that use the idiom below in a unique way.

Idiom: Birds of a feather flock together

One Idiom: Three Situations

Develop and perform three short scenes that use the idiom below in a unique way.

Idiom: Keep your head above water

One Idiom: Three Situations

Develop and perform three short scenes that use the idiom below in a unique way.

Idiom: Where there's smoke, there's fire

One, Two, Three, Go!

This improvisation game requires students to use three random idioms in one scene. Divide students into groups of four or five. Challenge groups to use their creative-thinking skills to come up with a scenario in which the three idioms make sense. (You can copy, cut out, and distribute the lists below.) Encourage students to link the idioms in truly creative and humorous ways. Each scene should last approximately one to two minutes. Read the three idioms to the class before each group's performance. (Variation: You can revisit this activity using five random spelling or vocabulary words.)

One, Two, Three, Go!
Develop a scene that uses these idioms.
Idiom 1: Make your mouth water
Idiom 2: Everything but the kitchen sink
Idiom 3: Poor as a church mouse

One, Two, Three, Go!
Develop a scene that uses these idioms.
Idiom 1: Hit the spot
Idiom 2: Cost an arm and a leg
Idiom 3: Kill two birds with one stone

One, Two, Three, Go!
Develop a scene that uses these idioms.
Idiom 1: Red-carpet treatment
Idiom 2: If the shoe fits, wear it
Idiom 3: Rotten apple spoils the barrel

One, Two, Three, Go!
Develop a scene that uses these idioms.
Idiom 1: Watched pot never boils
Idiom 2: Like two peas in a pod
Idiom 3: Out of sight, out of mind

One, Two, Three, Go!
Develop a scene that uses these idioms.
Idiom 1: Old wives' tale
Idiom 2: Skating on thin ice
Idiom 3: By the skin of your teeth

One, Two, Three, Go!
Develop a scene that uses these idioms.
Idiom 1: Where there's smoke, there's fire
Idiom 2: Straight from the horse's mouth
Idiom 3: Sight for sore eyes

One, Two, Three, Go!
Develop a scene that uses these idioms.
Idiom 1: On pins and needles
Idiom 2: Every cloud has a silver lining
Idiom 3: Make a mountain out of a molehill

One, Two, Three, Go!
Develop a scene that uses these idioms.
Idiom 1: Up a creek without a paddle
Idiom 2: Blood is thicker than water
Idiom 3: Early bird catches the worm

Like Two Peas in a Pod

Many idioms go together "like two peas in a pod" because they
have the same basic meanings. Write each idiom from the list
below in the square with the idiom that shares its meaning.

♦ **Bite the bullet**

♦ **Butterflies in the stomach**

♦ **Chip off the old block**

♦ **Don't open a can of worms**

♦ **Everything but the kitchen sink**

♦ **Go over with a fine-tooth comb**

♦ **If at first you don't succeed, try, try again**

♦ **Let the cat out of the bag**

♦ **Make hay while the sun shines**

♦ **On cloud nine**

♦ **Up a creek without a paddle**

♦ **Wild-goose chase**

1. Face the music	**7.** On top of the world
2. Needle in a haystack	**8.** On pins and needles
3. From soup to nuts	**9.** Rome was not built in a day
4. In the doghouse	**10.** Spill the beans
5. Leave no stone unturned	**11.** Spitting image
6. Let sleeping dogs lie	**12.** Strike while the iron is hot

Name _____ Date _____

Birds of a Feather Flock Together

Many idioms flock together "like birds of a feather" because they have the same basic meanings. Write each idiom from the list below in the square with the idiom that shares its meaning.

- ♦ **Bats in your belfry**
- ♦ **Go against the grain**
- ♦ **Take a backseat**
- ♦ **Hit the roof**
- ♦ **Cost an arm and a leg**
- ♦ **Rock the boat**

- ♦ **Don't count your chickens before they've hatched**
- ♦ **Shoot the breeze**
- ♦ **Go fly a kite**
- ♦ **Out of the clear blue sky**
- ♦ **In the driver's seat**
- ♦ **That's the way the ball bounces**

1.	Blow your stack	**7.**	Off your rocker
2.	Call the shots	**8.**	Pay through the nose
3.	Chew the fat	**9.**	Play second fiddle
4.	Don't put the cart before the horse	**10.**	Rub the wrong way
5.	Go jump in a lake	**11.**	That's the way the cookie crumbles
6.	Make waves	**12.**	Bolt from the blue

20 Hands-On Activities for Learning Idioms Scholastic Professional Books

Scrambled Idioms

All of the idioms below have been cut in half.
Match each beginning to its proper ending by
writing an ending from the box on the correct line.

be choosers	run deep
come home	skin a cat
come to it	spite your face
eat it too	spoil the broth
fly right	spoil the child
fry an egg	swim
hatch	throw stones
make him drink	

1. Go _____

2. There's more than one way to _____

3. Don't count your chickens before they _____

4. Too many cooks _____

5. Still waters _____

6. Have your cake and _____

7. You can lead a horse to water but you can't _____

8. Straighten up and _____

9. Cross that bridge when you _____

10. Sink or _____

11. People who live in glass houses shouldn't _____

12. Spare the rod and _____

13. Till the cows _____

14. Cut off your nose to _____

15. Beggars can't _____

Idioms by the Numbers

Write a number on each of the lines below in order to complete these numerical idioms. The answers can be found down the sides of the page. Each answer will be used once. Hint: Cross off each number as you use it.

10

1

2

q

6

1

1,000

1

5

2

5

8

½

2

40

11

q

2

4

1

1. _____ of one and a half dozen of the other

2. On cloud _____

3. _____-horse town

4. Behind the _____ ball

5. _____ winks

6. _____ good turn deserves another

7. _____-faced

8. Better _____

9. Goody-_____-shoes

10. _____ corners of the Earth

11. Give me _____

12. Dressed to the _____s

13. Cast the _____st stone

14. Touch something with a _____-foot pole

15. It takes _____ to tango

16. _____th hour

17. _____th wheel

18. A Picture is worth _____ words

19. Play _____nd fiddle

20. _____-track mind

20 Hands-On Activities for Learning Idioms Scholastic Professional Books

Glossary

The following is an alphabetical list of all the idioms mentioned in this book. Many of the meanings come from the *Scholastic Dictionary of Idioms* by Marvin Terban (Scholastic, 1996), which features over six hundred idioms, their meanings, and their origins.

A

Add fuel to the fire to make a bad situation worse; to do or say something that causes more trouble, makes someone angrier

Air your dirty laundry in public to talk about your private disagreements or embarrassing matters in public, usually while quarreling

Albatross around your neck a very difficult burden that you can't get rid of or a reminder of something you did that was wrong

All ears eager to listen; sharply attentive; curious

All thumbs awkward and clumsy, especially with the hands

Ants in your pants extreme restlessness; overactivity

Apple of your eye a person or thing that is greatly loved, treasured, and adored

As the crow flies by the shortest and most direct route; measured in a straight, direct line between two places

Asleep at the switch not attending to one's job or failing to react quickly; not being alert

At the end of your rope at the limit of your ability, endurance, or patience to do something

B

Babe in the woods a person who is inexperienced; a naive, trusting person

Back to square one return to the beginning because of a failure to accomplish the desired result

Backseat driver a bossy person who tells another person what to do; a person who gives unwanted advice and directions

Bark is worse than your bite the way a person sounds is much more frightening than the way she or he acts; the threat is often worse than the action taken

Barking up the wrong tree to direct your attention or efforts toward the wrong person or thing; to have the wrong idea about something

Bats in your belfry a person who has crazy ideas or acts irrationally

Beat a dead horse to pursue a useless goal; to continue fighting a battle which has been lost; to keep arguing a point which has already been decided

Beauty is in the eye of the beholder there is no standard for beauty, so what one person likes or sees in someone or something is not necessarily what others see; different people have different opinions

Bee in your bonnet a crazy idea; an obsession with an idea

Beggars can't be choosers needy people have to take whatever they can get and cannot be concerned about the quality if they cannot afford to buy it for themselves

Behind the eight ball in trouble or out of luck; in a difficult position or in a bad situation with little hope of winning

Below par unsatisfactory; below expectations

Better half either partner in marriage

Between a rock and a hard place being in a very tight spot and faced with a difficult decision

Bird in the hand is worth two in the bush what you already have is better than what you might or might not get in the future; a guarantee is worth more than a promise

Birds of a feather flock together people who have things in common, such as interests and ideas, usually hang out together; people who are alike often become friends

Bite off more than you can chew to take on a task that is more than you can accomplish; to be greedy, overconfident, or too ambitious by taking on more jobs or responsibilities than you can deal with at one time

Bite the bullet prepare for an unpleasant experience; brace yourself to endure with courage something painful but necessary

Bite the dust to die; to fall in defeat; to fail to succeed

Bite the hand that feeds you to turn against someone who helps you; to do harm to someone who does good things for you

Black sheep of the family the most unsuccessful, least admirable member of a family or similar group; a disgraced person

Bleeding heart an extremely softhearted person who feels compassion or pity towards all people, including those who may not deserve sympathy

Blood is thicker than water one can expect more kindness from a family member than from a stranger; a person will do more for a relative than for anyone else

Blow your stack see *Hit the roof*

Blue blood of high or noble birth; an aristocrat; from the upper class of society

Bolt from the blue something sudden, unexpected, and shocking

Born with a silver spoon in your mouth born to wealth, comfort, and privilege

Bowl of cherries a wonderful, pleasant situation or position; an easy, comfortable life

Bring down the house to get an audience to clap enthusiastically or laugh loudly

Bug off to leave someone alone; go away; stop annoying someone

Bull in a china shop a clumsy person who deals too roughly with a delicate situation; a rough person who is near breakable things; a tactless person who says or does something that angers people or upsets their plans

Burn the candle at both ends to overwork yourself mentally or physically and until you're exhausted

Burn the midnight oil to stay up very late at night studying or working

Burn your bridges behind you to make a decision you cannot change; to commit oneself to a course of action

Burn yourself out to exhaust yourself by overworking physically or mentally

Bury your head in the sand to ignore danger by pretending you don't see it; to hide from obvious signs of danger

Busy as a beaver working very hard; extremely industrious

Busy as a bee see *Busy as a beaver*

Butter someone up to flatter someone; to try to get a favor by praising someone

Butterflies in the stomach a fluttery feeling in the stomach, usually caused by nervousness

Button your lip to stop talking; be quiet

Buy a pig in a poke to buy something without seeing or examining it

By the skin of your teeth by an extremely narrow margin; with practically no room to spare; just barely

C

Call it a day to stop work for the day; to bring a project to an end for the time being

Call the shots to make the decisions; to be in charge; to give orders

Can't see the forest for the trees to overlook the overall situation because of a focus on small details; to be so involved in details that you miss the whole picture

Cast the first stone to be the first to attack, blame, or criticize someone; to lead accusers against a wrongdoer

Cat got your tongue? Is there a reason that you're not speaking?

Catch someone red-handed to catch someone in the act of doing something wrong

Chew the fat to have a friendly, informal talk; to chat in a relaxed way

Chew up the scenery to overact; to exaggerate your emotions

Chicken feed a very small or insignificant amount of money

Chickens come home to roost words or actions come back to haunt a person; evil acts will return to plague the doer

Chip off the old block a child who resembles a parent in behavior, looks, or abilities

Clean as a hound's tooth completely free from dirt; perfectly neat (also *Clean as a whistle*)

Climb the walls to be frustrated or anxious during a challenging situation; to be unable to endure

Cold turkey the sudden stopping of any habit

Come up smelling like a rose to get out of a possibly embarrassing or disgraceful situation without hurting your reputation, and maybe even improving it

Cook your goose to put an end to; to ruin someone's plans

Cool as a cucumber very calm; not nervous or emotional

Cost an arm and a leg very expensive; high-priced, though possibly not worth the cost

Crocodile tears fake tears; false grief

Cross that bridge when you come to it don't predict problems until they actually happen; don't worry about future events now; don't deal with a difficulty until you have to

Cut off your nose to spite your face to injure yourself out of anger toward another; to make a situation worse for yourself when angry with someone

D

Dark-horse candidate a contestant about whom little is known and who wins unexpectedly

Dead as a dodo totally dead or hopeless; without a chance of success (also *Dead as a doornail*)

Dead duck a person who is ruined; a person or project unlikely to continue or survive

Dog days of summer the hottest and most humid days of summer, usually much of July and August

Dog-eat-dog world a way of life marked by fierce competition in which people compete ruthlessly for survival or success

Dog's life a bleak, harsh, terrible existence without much happiness or freedom

Don't count your chickens before they hatch don't count on profits before you earn them or have them in hand

Don't look a gift horse in the mouth don't complain if a gift is not perfect; take what you've been given without criticism or emphasis on its worth

Down in the mouth sad and depressed (also *Down in the dumps*)

Down the drain lost forever; wasted

Down the hatch swallow a drink in one gulp

Down-to-the-wire running out of time; at the very last minute

Dressed to the nines wearing fashionable clothing; dressed to attract attention

Drive you up the wall to make someone angry or confused; to make somebody very annoyed or frustrated

Drop you like a hot potato to get rid of something or somebody as quickly as possible

E

Eager beaver see *Busy as a beaver*

Early bird catches the worm a person who gets up early and starts a project ahead of others has the best chance of accomplishing his or her goal

Eat crow to be forced to do something very disagreeable; to acknowledge a mistake or defeat

Eat your heart out to feel extremely unhappy about a hopeless situation; to make yourself sick with grief and worry

Eat your words to have to take back what you said; to admit humbly that you were wrong

Elbow grease hard, energetic manual labor

Eleventh hour at the latest possible time, just before the absolute deadline

Every cloud has a silver lining there is something good in every bad situation

Everything but the kitchen sink practically everything there is; every possible object whether needed or not

Eye for an eye and a tooth for a tooth revenge or punishment exactly like the original crime or offense

Eyes in the back of your head ability to sense what is happening outside one's field of vision; ability to know what happens when one's back is turned

F

Face the music to endure the consequences of one's actions; to take what you have coming to you

Fat cat a wealthy person; a rich benefactor

Feel your oats to be in high spirits, energetic; to act in a proud way

Field day to have unlimited opportunities; to have it all your own way; to go all out and experience success at something

Fifth wheel an unneeded, extra person

Fish or cut bait do one thing or another, but stop delaying; make a choice; act now or give someone else a turn

Fish out of water a person who is out of his or her usual place; someone who doesn't fit in or is helpless in a situation

Fly by the seat of your pants to do something by instinct and feel without any earlier experience or instruction

Fly in the ointment a small annoyance that spoils an otherwise pleasant situation

Foam at the mouth to be uncontrollably furious, like a mad dog

Follow your nose to go straight ahead in the same direction

For the birds worthless; useless; stupid

Forty winks a short nap

Four corners of the Earth from all over the planet; all parts of a place

From soup to nuts the whole thing from beginning to end

Full of beans lively, happy and energetic, high-spirited

Full of hot air being foolish and talking nonsense; pompous; vain

G

Get a kick out of something to enjoy doing something; to get a thrill out of something

Get the pink slip to be fired

Get under your skin to bother or upset someone

Get your goat to annoy very badly; to make a person angry

Get your walking papers to be fired

Give me five to slap a person's hand as a hearty greeting or a sign of solid agreement

Give your eyeteeth for something to want something very badly; to be willing to give up something valuable to get something else

Go against the grain to oppose natural tendencies; to oppose a person's wishes or feelings; to cause anger

Go along for the ride to watch but not take part in an activity; to keep someone company

Go bananas to be or go crazy

Go climb a tree go away; leave; stop bothering me

Go fly a kite see *Go climb a tree*

Go fry an egg see *Go climb a tree*

Go jump in a lake see *Go climb a tree*

Go over like a lead balloon to fail miserably

Go over with a fine-tooth comb to search with great care or attention

Go to the dogs to decline in looks or health; to be ruined or destroyed; to ruin oneself

Go yellow to act cowardly

Gone to pot become ruined; to get worse and worse

Goody-two-shoes a person who thinks he or she is perfect and tries to be

Green thumb having a special talent for making flowers and green plants grow well

Green with envy extremely jealous

H

Hand-to-mouth existence to spend your salary as fast as it's earned without saving any for the future

Hard nut to crack a problem that's very difficult to understand or solve; a difficult person

Have other fish to fry to have other things to do; to not bother with one thing because you have more important things to accomplish

Have your cake and eat it too to spend or use something up but still have it; to have two things when you must choose one

Have your heart in your mouth to be extremely frightened about something

Head and shoulders above someone far superior; much better than

Head in the clouds absent-minded; daydreaming; lost in thought

Heart's in the right place to be well-meaning and kindhearted; to have good intentions even though mistakes occur

High horse acting superior and arrogant as if you were better than other people

Hit below the belt to use unfair tactics or be unsportsmanlike

Hit the books study school assignments carefully; prepare for classes by reading and doing homework

Hit the road to begin a journey, to leave

Hit the roof to lose your temper suddenly; to become violently angry

Hit the spot to fully satisfy and refresh, especially with food or drink

Hold your horses slow down; wait a minute; be patient

Hold your tongue struggle not to say something you want to say

Horse of a different color a different matter altogether; something from a different nature from that being noticed

Hot under the collar very angry; upset

I

If at first you don't succeed, try, try again don't give up; if you make a mistake you should keep working at it until you are successful

If the shoe fits, wear it If a remark applies to you, you should admit that it is true.

In a pickle see *Behind the eight ball*

In hot water in serious trouble or in an embarrassing situation with someone of authority

In the doghouse in disgrace or dislike; facing punishment

In the driver's seat in control; in the position of authority

In the pink in excellent health physically and emotionally

It takes two to tango two people are required to accomplish this deed

J

Jump down your throat to talk or scream at someone in a sudden, angry way

Jump on the bandwagon to become part of the newest activity because many other people are

K

Keep something under your hat to keep something secret

Keep your ear to the ground to pay attention and be well-informed

Keep your fingers crossed to wish for good luck and success for someone or something

Keep your head above water to earn enough to stay out of debt and avoid financial ruin; to do just enough to keep up with all of one's responsibilities

Keep your nose to the grindstone to force oneself to work hard all the time; to always keep busy

Kill the goose that lays the golden eggs to spoil or destroy something good out of stupidity, greed, or impatience

Kill two birds with one stone to do two things by one action; to get two results with just one effort

Knee-high to a grasshopper very young and, therefore, very short

L

Laugh out of the other side of your mouth to be made to feel sorrow, annoyance, or disappointment after you felt happy; to cry at a change in luck after experiencing some happiness

Lay an egg to give an embarrassing performance

Leave no stone unturned to make all possible efforts to carry out a task or search for someone or something

Lend an ear to listen and pay attention to

Let sleeping dogs lie to not make trouble if you don't have to; to not make someone angry by stirring up trouble

Let the cat out of the bag to give away a secret

Like two peas in a pod identical; alike in looks and behavior

Little pitchers have big ears little children, listening to the conversations of older people, often hear and understand a lot more than people give them credit for

Live high off the hog to live in a rich style and own lots of expensive things

Lock the barn door after the horse is out to take careful precautions to do the right thing after it is too late

Long in the tooth old; aged

Look down your nose at someone to think of and treat people as if they were lower in quality or ability

Look what the cat dragged in a person who looks disheveled; the arrival of an unwanted person

M

Mad as a wet hen very upset; extremely angry; ready to fight

Make a mountain out of a molehill to turn a small, unimportant issue into a big, important one; to exaggerate the importance of something

Make a silk purse out of a sow's ear to create something valuable or beautiful out of something practically worthless or ugly

Make hay while the sun shines to make the best of a limited opportunity

Make it by a nose to succeed at the very last moment

Make waves to cause trouble; to upset matters; to create a disturbance

Make your mouth water to look so attractive and desirable that it makes you want to have it very much; to want to eat or drink something that looks or smells delicious

Monkey business silliness or fooling around; dishonest or illegal activities; idiotic pranks

More than meets the eye there are hidden facts that can't be seen or understood right away

More than one way to skin a cat there are several different ways of reaching the same goal

N

Name is mud the person is in trouble, possibly doomed and worthless

Need something like a hole in the head to have no need for something at all

Need something like a third leg see *Need something like a hole in the head*

Needle in a haystack something hard or impossible to find; anything hopeless (in a search)

No skin off your nose of totally no concern to you whatsoever; it doesn't matter to you one way or the other

No spring chicken not young anymore

O

Off the beaten track (path) not well-known or used; an unfamiliar location; unusual; different

Off the top of your head stating something quickly and without thinking hard about it

Off-the-wall shocking; very unusual

Off your rocker crazy; silly, foolish; not thinking correctly

Old wives' tale a superstition; a belief or practice not based on fact

On cloud nine blissfully happy; joyous

On pins and needles waiting anxiously for something; extremely nervous; in great suspense

On the ball alert; effective; skillful; knowledgeable

On top of the world feeling extremely happy

Once bitten, twice shy when something bad happens to you, you will think twice before putting yourself in the same situation

Once in a blue moon almost never; very seldom; hardly ever

One good turn deserves another one good deed should be paid back with another

One-horse town a place with few comforts and activities; a dull rural town

One-track mind always thinking about only one subject

Open a can of worms to cause trouble; to set unpleasant events in motion

Out in left field unusual; crazy; totally wrong

Out of sight, out of mind if you don't see something for a long time, you'll eventually stop thinking about it

Out of the clear blue sky suddenly and without any warning; totally unexpectedly

Out of the frying pan and into the fire from a bad situation into one that is worse

Out of the mouths of babes children can unexpectedly say very intelligent things

Out of the woods safe from trouble or danger

Out on a limb taking a chance; in a dangerous position from which it is hard to withdraw or change

Over a barrel helpless; in someone's power; at a disadvantage

Over the hill past one's prime; unable to function as one used to; too old

Over your head a risky situation that will lead to certain failure; beyond your ability to understand something

P

Pay through the nose to pay too much for something

People who live in glass houses shouldn't throw stones you should not criticize others if you are just as bad as they are

Picture is worth a thousand words to actually see or experience something is much better than to merely have it described to you

Pie in the sky something not possible; an unrealistic hope

Play both ends against the middle to pit two opponents against each other in such a way as to benefit yourself; to use each of two sides for your own purpose

Play cat and mouse to fool or tease someone by pretending to let her or him go free and then catching her or him again

Play second fiddle to be a follower; to be in an inferior position

Play with fire to take an unnecessary and dangerous risk; to court danger

Poor as a church mouse very poor; poverty-stricken

Pot calling the kettle black the person criticizing another person's faults is guilty of the same faults himself or herself

Power behind the throne the actual, but unrecognized, person in charge

Pull a rabbit out of a hat to produce something that is needed as if by magic; to unexpectedly find a solution to a problem

Pull the wool over your eyes to fool, deceive, or trick someone

Pull your leg to tease or fool someone; to jokingly try to lie to somebody

Pull yourself together to regain control over one's emotions and become calm after being very upset

Put all your ducks in a row to organize or finish things before moving on to something else

Put the cart before the horse to do things in the wrong order

Put your money where your mouth is to be willing to bet on or invest your money in something you support or believe in

Q

Quick on the draw ready, alert, and quick to respond or react; mentally fast; quick to grasp information; touchy, sensitive

Quiet as a mouse silent or still; making very little noise; saying nothing; hushed, subdued

R

Raining cats and dogs to rain very heavily; to pour

Raise the roof to be very angry, complain loudly, and make trouble

Rat race a fierce, unending, stressful competition in business or society

Rats abandoning a sinking ship disloyal people who desert a failing enterprise before it's too late

Read between the lines to discern the true, hidden meaning or fact in any document or action

Red-carpet treatment great respect and hospitality given to someone important; special treatment

Red herring something deliberately misleading to divert your attention from the main subject; something irrelevant that confuses an issue

Red-letter day a day remembered as especially happy and significant

Red tape excessive formality and time-consuming, rigid adherence to rules and regulations

Right off the bat immediately, spontaneously, and without delay

Rock the boat to make trouble and disrupt a stable situation; to risk spoiling a plan; to create a disturbance

Rome was not built in a day a difficult or important goal or task cannot be achieved quickly or all at once

Rotten apple spoils the barrel one bad person or thing may spoil an entire group

Rub the wrong way to annoy and irritate someone; to handle someone insensitively

Run circles around someone to easily do something far better than someone else

Run off at the mouth to talk too much; to talk nonstop

S

Save for a rainy day to save for a time of need; to put something away for the future

Saved by the bell rescued at the last possible moment from an embarrassing or dangerous situation

Scarce as hen's teeth very, very rare or totally nonexistent

See eye to eye to agree fully; to have the same opinion

See a pink elephant to get so drunk you see things that don't exist

Sell like hotcakes to sell quickly, effortlessly, and in quantity

Seventh heaven being in an emotional state of extreme happiness

Shake a leg to hurry up; to go faster; to speed up

Shoot the breeze see *Chew the fat*

Sick as a dog very sick; suffering miserably without an ailment

Sight for sore eyes a most welcome, unexpected sight; a pleasant surprise

Sink or swim to fail or succeed by one's own efforts without anyone's help or interference

Sitting duck someone or something likely to be attacked and unable to put up a defense

Six of one and a half dozen of the other one and the same; nothing to choose between; equal

Skate on thin ice to take a big chance; to risk danger; to start out on a hazardous course of action

Skeleton in your closet a shameful and shocking secret that people try to keep hidden

Smell a rat to be suspicious; to feel that something is wrong

Smell something fishy see *Smell a rat*

Snug as a bug in a rug cozy and comfortable; safe and secure

Spare the rod and spoil the child to physically punish children when they misbehave so they'll learn to behave properly in the future

Spill the beans to give away a secret to someone who is not supposed to know it

Spitting image a perfect resemblance; an exact likeness

Still waters run deep somebody can be more knowledgeable or emotional than he or she first appears to be; a silent person may be intelligent

Stir up a hornet's nest to make many people furious; to cause trouble

Straight from the horse's mouth directly from the person or place that is the most reliable source or the best authority

Straighten up and fly right to stop behaving foolishly and start acting serious

Strike a happy medium to find a compromise to a problem; to find a sensible solution midway between two opposite desires

Strike while the iron is hot to act at the most favorable time or moment to get the best results; to take advantage of favorable conditions

Swallow hook, line, and sinker to believe a story completely without questioning it; to be very gullible

Swan song the final, farewell performance of an actor or singer; one's last words or actions

Sweep you off your feet to make a favorable impression; to affect with strong emotion or enthusiasm; to overcome someone with feelings of love or happiness so strong that he or she can't resist you

T

Take a backseat to be in an inferior position; to take second place to another person who is in control

Take someone under your wing to help, guide, or protect someone

Take the bull by the horns to act bravely in a troublesome situation; to face up to a difficult challenge by taking decisive action

That's the way the ball bounces that's the way life is; that's fate; things sometimes turn out a certain way and you can't do anything about it

That's the way the cookie crumbles see *That's the way the ball bounces*

Throw a monkey wrench into the works to interfere with a smoothly running operation; to upset something in progress

Throw the baby out with the bathwater to lose or throw out something valuable or useful when getting rid of something that is useless

Throw the book at someone to punish severely for breaking rules or the law; to give the maximum penalty

Tickled pink to be very amused or pleased; to be delighted, entertained, or extremely happy

Till the cows come home for a long, long time

Too many cooks spoil the broth a project is set back rather than helped by too many organizers; the more people who work on one project, the worse it will turn out

Top banana the leading comedian in a variety show; a boss

Touch and go very risky, uncertain, or critical

Touch something with a ten-foot pole to avoid at all costs; to stay far away from a difficult problem

True-blue very loyal, dependable, and faithful

Turn up your nose at someone to regard something with haughtiness; to be snobby; to show that someone or something is not good enough for you

Two-faced false; dishonest

Two's company, three's a crowd when you would like to do something with just one other person, a third participant would be unwelcome

U

Up a creek without a paddle in deep trouble and unable to do anything about it; in serious trouble

Up against the wall in big trouble; in a difficult or desperate situation

Upset the applecart to spoil or interfere with a plan; to obstruct progress; to mess everything up by surprise or accident

W

Walk on eggs to be very cautious; to proceed warily

Walking on air to be exuberantly happy, excited, and joyful

Watched pot never boils when waiting anxiously or impatiently for something to happen, it seems to take much longer

Water under the bridge something that happened in the past; it's too late to worry about something that already happened

Wear your heart on your sleeve to show one's emotions and feelings openly

Wet behind the ears young, inexperienced, and immature

What's good for the goose is good for the gander a rule or method of treatment that applies to one person or group must also apply to others, especially your mate

When the cat's away, the mice will play when the person in charge is absent, people will usually do as they please and take advantage of the freedom

Where there's smoke, there's fire there is always a basis for a rumor, no matter how untrue it appears; suspicious things usually mean that something is wrong

White elephant any possession that is useless, unwanted, or costs a lot of money to keep

Wild-goose chase a useless or hopeless search, especially because something does not exist or can't be found

Wolf in sheep's clothing somebody who appears to be harmless but is really dangerous

Word of mouth by one person telling another; by speaking, rather than writing

Y

You can lead a horse to water but you can't make him drink you can encourage, but not force, someone to do something

You can't teach an old dog new tricks people who find it difficult or impossible to change their ways or adjust to new ideas

Z

Zipper your mouth see *Button your lip*

Answers

Page 51
1. Bite the bullet
2. Wild-goose chase
3. Everything but the kitchen sink
4. Up the creek without a paddle
5. Go over with a fine-tooth comb
6. Don't open a can of worms
7. On cloud nine
8. Butterflies in the stomach
9. If at first you don't succeed, try, try again
10. Let the cat out of the bag
11. Chip off the old block
12. Make hay while the sun shines

Page 52
1. Hit the roof
2. In the driver's seat
3. Shoot the breeze
4. Don't count your chickens before they've hatched
5. Go fly a kite
6. Rock the boat
7. Bats in your belfry
8. Cost an arm and a leg
9. Take a backseat
10. Go against the grain
11. That's the way the ball bounces
12. Out of the clear blue sky

Page 53
1. fry an egg
2. skin a cat
3. hatch
4. spoil the broth
5. run deep
6. eat it too
7. make him drink
8. fly right
9. come to it
10. swim
11. throw stones
12. spoil the child
13. come home
14. spite your face
15. be choosers

Page 54
1. 6
2. 9
3. 1
4. 8
5. 40
6. 1
7. 2
8. ½
9. 2
10. 4
11. 5
12. 9
13. 1
14. 10
15. 2
16. 11
17. 5
18. 1,000
19. 2
20. 1